D0819693

# Which One Doesn't Belong?

## And Other Puzzles From Sesame Street

by Linda Hayward

Illustrated by Kimberly A. McSparran

Featuring Jim Henson's
Sesame Street Muppets

A SESAME STREET / GOLDEN PRESS BOOK
Published by Western Publishing Company, Inc.
in conjunction with Children's Television Workshop.

© 1981 Children's Television Workshop.
Muppet characters © 1981 Muppets, Inc. All rights reserved. Printed in U.S.A.
SESAME STREET®, the SESAME STREET SIGN, and SESAME STREET BOOK CLUB are trademarks
and service marks of Children's Television Workshop. GOLDEN® and GOLDEN PRESS® are trademarks of
Western Publishing Company, Inc. No part of this book may be reproduced or copied in any form without
written permission from the publisher. Library of Congress Catalog Card Number: 80-83290
ISBN 0-307-23127-5

Big Bird and Little Bird are getting wet.
They need some clothes to keep them dry.
Point to the things that will fit Big Bird.
Point to the things that will fit Little Bird.

What's missing?

What's missing now?

What's missing this time?

Which cookie looks like the square cookie cutter?
Which cookie looks like the circle cookie cutter?
Which cookie looks like the heart cookie cutter?
Which cookie looks like the star cookie cutter?

Betty Lou is inviting a friend to come over and play.
Who is Betty Lou calling?
Put your finger on Betty Lou's telephone.
Now follow the wire until you come to another telephone.
The Count's pet cat is caught in a tree. Who is the Count calling?
Mr. Snuffle-upagus is inviting his best friend over for spaghetti.
Who is Snuffie calling?

Ernie made a peanut butter sandwich.
Which picture shows what Ernie did first?
Which picture shows what Ernie did last?

Which pictures show Grover riding?

Which hat is different?

Which shoes are different?

Which pigeon is different?

Who has a suitcase full of things to wear?
Who has a suitcase full of things to eat?
Who has a suitcase full of things
    to play with?

Which thing belongs in Ernie's suitcase?
Which thing belongs in Bert's suitcase?
Which thing belongs in Cookie's suitcase?

Farmer Grover is huffing and puffing and puffing and huffing but he cannot push his wheelbarrow down the road. Can you see why?
Can you find two more things that are wrong in this picture?

# Which Twiddlebug is doing something different —

at the playground?
at the library?

Find the two ladders.
Find the two mirrors.
Find the two clocks.

Can you find any more pairs?

Betty Lou built a new house for Barkley.
She made the house with one door.
She also made one mistake. What mistake did she make?
Now find the place where each tool belongs.

## Which one of these things doesn't belong?

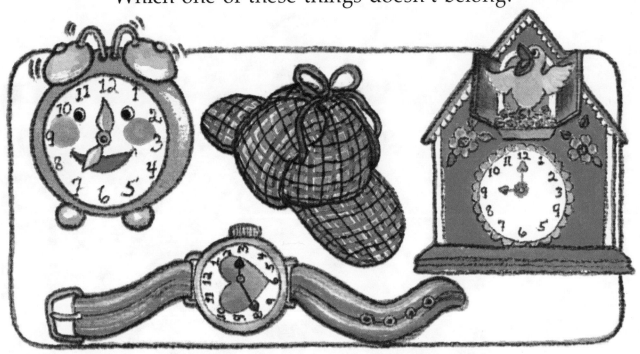

## Which one of these things doesn't belong?

How many 5's can you find?

Slimey has his own little house under the ground
where he likes to sleep and eat and watch TV.
Help Slimey get to his house.
Use your finger to trace his path.

Which contestant has something that rhymes with CLOCK?

Which contestant has something that rhymes with PEAR?

Which contestant has something that rhymes with HAT?

What's missing?

What's missing?

What's missing?

What belongs in Bert's collection of BROWN THINGS?
What belongs in Bert's collection of GRAY THINGS?
What belongs in Bert's collection of PINK THINGS?
Which box is the box for them?

Once upon a time there were three
monsters — a Great Big Monster,
a Middle-Sized Monster,
and a Wee Little Monster.

One day they went to the beach. Each monster
took a pail and shovel. The Great Big Monster took
a great big pail and shovel. The Middle-Sized
Monster took a middle-sized pail and shovel. And
the Wee Little Monster took a wee little pail and
shovel.

Which pail and shovel belong to each monster?

When they arrived at the beach, each monster built a sand castle. The Great Big Monster built a great big sand castle. The Middle-Sized Monster built a middle-sized sand castle. And the Wee Little Monster built a wee little sand castle.

Which sand castle was built by each monster?

Then each monster sat down in a beach chair. The Great Big Monster sat down in a great big beach chair. The Middle-Sized Monster sat down in a middle-sized beach chair. And the Wee Little Monster sat down in a wee little beach chair.

Which beach chair belongs to each monster?

Then the three monsters went for a swim. While they were gone, Betty Lou came to deliver sandwiches from the sandwich store.

"Oh, dear," she said. "I have a great big salami sandwich and a middle-sized bologna sandwich and a wee little pastrami sandwich, and I don't know whom to deliver them to."

Just then the three monsters came out of the water.

Do *you* know what sandwich belongs to which monster?

ABCDEFGHIJK